A Real Man Would Have a Gun

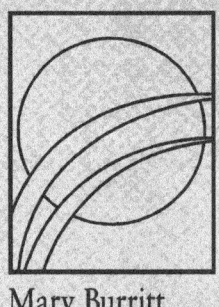

Mary Burritt
      Christiansen
Poetry Series

Mary Burritt Christiansen Poetry Series
Hilda Raz, Series Editor

The Mary Burritt Christiansen Poetry Series publishes two to four books a year that engage and give voice to the realities of living, working, and experiencing the West and the Border as places and as metaphors. The purpose of the series is to expand access to, and the audience for, quality poetry, both single volumes and anthologies, that can be used for general reading as well as in classrooms.

Also available in the Mary Burritt Christiansen Poetry Series:

For additional titles in the Mary Burritt Christiansen Poetry Series, please visit unmpress.com.

A Real Man Would Have a Gun

Poems

Stacey Waite

University of New Mexico Press | Albuquerque

Library of Congress Cataloging-in-Publication Data

Names: Waite, Stacey, author.

Title: A real man would have a gun: poems / Stacey
Waite. Other titles: Mary Burritt Christiansen poetry
series.

Description: Albuquerque: University of New Mexico
Press, 2025. | Series: Mary Burritt Christiansen poetry
series.

Identifiers: LCCN 2024024799 (print) | LCCN
2024024800 (ebook) | ISBN 9780826367488
(paperback) | ISBN 9780826367495 (epub).

Subjects: LCGFT: Poetry.

Classification: LCC PS3623.A356558 R43 2025 (print)
| LCC PS3623.A356558 (ebook) | DDC 811/.6--dc23/
eng/20240610.

LC record available at https://lccn.loc.gov/2024024799.

LC ebook record available at https://lccn.loc.
gov/2024024800

Founded in 1889, the University of New Mexico sits on
the traditional homelands of the Pueblo of Sandia. The
original peoples of New Mexico—Pueblo, Navajo, and
Apache—since time immemorial have deep connections
to the land and have made significant contributions
to the broader community statewide. We honor the
land itself and those who remain stewards of this land
throughout the generations and also acknowledge our
committed relationship to Indigenous peoples. We
gratefully recognize our history.

Cover image courtesy of Gabriel Jesiolowski
Designed by Isaac Morris
Composed in Input Serif, and Jenson Pro

For Max and Ollie

Contents

Part One

Part Two

Part Three

A Real Man Would Have a Gun

Part One

Honest Poem

after Rudy Francisco

I was born in 1977, the same year
Voyager 1 was launched into space,
soon to discover two new Jovian moons.
I like excessive levels of air conditioning,
New York bagels, and the sound of my kids
jumping into the inflatable pool in the yard.
I've been told I'm a people person, but
the truth is I've never been good at letting
anyone see me tired or weak or full
of the childhood rage that even four years
of EMDR therapy has only turned into
a fire of a different kind. I've never been
much good at girl things, but sometimes
when I am doing the Cupid Shuffle
with my four-year-old daughter, I think
I should have danced more, should have
learned to braid hair or paint fingernails.
My mother was an alcoholic, not the raging kind,
but the kind who believes loving a child means
there is nothing they could do that isn't perfect.
Sometimes I wish I believed in time travel.
Sometimes I am so afraid of dying
it keeps me up at night, and my worry
is strange and cyclical. I might wake up
at 3 a.m. thinking about whether
this poem is any good, and after
an hour of one spiraling thought
after another, I always end up dead,
which is another way of saying alone.
And isn't that what I've been avoiding
all these years—the dead hum sound
of no one else in the room, the terror
of my own body, the lump in my throat,
a small moon I want no part of finding?

Mothers and Men

My mother never warned me of anything,
never said, "Watch out for boys who
spit or curse or punch,"
never said, "Look for signs
he needs to control you,"
never said, "Boys will be boys,"
never said, "Beware the brute strength
of big men." Maybe she thought I might
be one of them, feared the part of me
that would not woman. And yet
I still wander off into the woods
with Joel at twelve, his tongue
rolling in my mouth like an avocado pit.
Then his whole hands close
around the bone of my wrists.
He pushes my head toward his belt.
He says, "I won't let you go until you do."
He is smiling when he says it.
We are the same height, Joel and I,
both our jawlines lean and sharp,
our eyebrows thick and wet from the heat.
I don't say anything. I just shove him,
run through the woods, pine needles
digging their needling ends
into the bottoms of my feet. I feel the
sting of who we might become, Joel
and I, two men in the woods, one of us
a warning, the other a woman, a fleeing fire.

Scar

The first one I remember on my forehead,
the crescent shape of it near my hairline,
the six stitches like an abandoned railyard.
I was six, and as good children
of alcoholics do, I was wearing a cape,
playing Superman in the living room,
diving from couch to chair and back to couch,
the savior complex already begun.

Lois Lane was atop the fireplace, and the living room rug
was lava, so what else could I do but try to make the jump
from the side table all the way to the recliner?
Lois was screaming after all and had no superpowers
beyond the often disregarded ones all women have,
but that's for another poem. This poem, this poem
is about children playing Superman, about the hero,
the rescuer, the child who tells themselves their power
knows no bounds, the child whose foot
catches the lamp on the side table, the child whose head
crashes full force into the corner of the coffee table.

It will be years before the child gives up the cape,
even though it makes everyone mad, saves
no one in the end because, of course, we are
only capable of saving ourselves—our scars
are reminders of who we were, of how easy it is
to fall, to fail, to untell the story of our own power,
which in the end is just a story, one just like this.

1986

"Papa Don't Preach" hit the billboards.
Our fathers said we couldn't listen to the song—
because of Madonna, because of pregnant
teens in white dresses. But we listened anyway,
two rebellious girls, one of us less than half a girl,
holding our hands over the boombox
as if it were a gas stove for cold hands,
waiting for the radio to play it so we could tape it.

We hoped they'd play it before my father got home,
before his keys jingled at the door like rusted windchimes.
We were best friends and nine
and already tired of being told what to do,
already grown stone sick of every cruel thing
our fathers did to keep us from
who we wished to become.

We are about to find out that he is already home,
already in the kitchen mad about the music,
mad about Lionel Richie and Billy Ocean
and Prince. But Madonna, Madonna is about
to take him over the raging edge.

When I think of the two girls, one of us less than half a girl,
I want to tell them to plug the headphones in,
to tape the song another day,
to slip out the sliding glass doors
and stay out long enough that he'd forget what he'd heard.

But the two nine-year-olds, they love
Madonna so much they wouldn't hear me.
They'd just hold their hands out over the tape deck,
wait for the opening notes of the song to arrive,
wait to be punished again for the things they love.

Masculinity I

You should just keep leaving.
Run again from attachment.
I've got a hunch you've lost something
in a fire. I have dreams of you:
a small boy running from a burning house,
looking back for that one thing
he wishes he'd taken. Perhaps
you can still take it now. Take more.
Take it all with you when you go.

The Four Nights She's Gone

I

The news says two rapists
escaped from the state penitentiary.
Your friend's husband comes over
for dinner. He teaches your son to jump
the sprinkler in the yard. You drink gin
on the back steps, talk like two men do.

He eats spaghetti at your table,
the light settling behind the trees.
He stays when your son begs
for a movie, and the three of you
stretch out on the couch, the TV
fervent with little penguins.
Your son touches his beard;
you want him to spend the night,
to stand watch at the door
in shifts with you, like soldiers.

You talk yourself down:

the rapists won't come here
you took thirteen years of martial arts
you know how to kill a man
they might not even be rapists

You do not ask him to stay.
You hear the helicopters overhead,
their lights scanning the neighborhood.
You scold yourself as you put your son to bed.
What kind of man are you?
Maybe your son does need a father
if you are scared of a town jailbreak.

You sing to him,
the same song your mother sung to you.
You wonder what song
a real man would sing
or if the kind of man
who guards the door
would sing at all.

II

You find out an alligator
has snatched a two-year-old boy
from a lagoon. They say
his father fought the alligator
for his boy; they say this time of year
is nesting season for the alligator,
guarding her young, protecting
the perimeter of her ninety eggs
until she hears a high pitch of noise
which signals she should uncover the nest.

You imagine yourself fighting
the alligator, your fists bloody
with the scrape of her claws
which, they say, are considered
lucky for gamblers. You imagine
you are able to kill the alligator,
that your rage is too great
even for a five-hundred-pound
reptile mother. You close your eyes.
You see yourself carrying your son
from the water, the alligator

floating at the edge, dead
instead of your son. Her young
left to be born lost. This
is what we do: imagine
our strength more holy,
our rage more pure,
our love some otherworldly force
impossible to contain, dangerous
and beyond measure.

III

The neighborhood
too quiet—its breath sucked
into summer heat.
Your son asleep too easily,
doesn't even call you back,
doesn't plea for one more song
at the edge of his bed.

You sit still in a kitchen chair,
planted like a push pin,
staring into half-eaten dinner.

You don't clean the dishes.
You don't make his lunch.
You don't write anything down.
You sit perfectly still like a child
who thinks, *if I don't move
then no one can see me.*

IV

You fall asleep on the couch
as you sometimes do when
she's out of town. 2 a.m.,
the air conditioning quits on you,
the neighbor's dog barking
at its back gate. You wake up sweating.

You pull the steak knife from under the couch
(you've been carrying it from room to room).
You think to yourself: *a real man would have a gun.*

This night in Orlando there is a real man
with a real gun who has just begun shooting
in a nightclub, on a dance floor, in a bathroom.
Presumably protecting whatever it is
he sees fit to defend. But it turns out,
in the end, not everything broken
in him—in us—is worth saving.

Queer Body in Summer, 1989

That July her body ceased
to be intelligible. She didn't
want to move any part
of her body. Everything pointed
to her nipples: shirts, swimsuits,
the boys on the youth baseball team
with whom she would no longer run.
How she envied them, free and boundless.

What she would have done for her body
to melt away slow like a stubborn snow.
But it was her role to
disappear while the others
became more clear to themselves.

If only she could intertwine her fingers
like a pile of sticks, pray hard enough
to make her hands timber for the fire
that would burn it all down,
bring me home to myself whole.

Karen Berry

I learned piano from Karen Berry,
who was shaped like a wire
and lived with six cats.
The cats left their cat marks
on her bony hands, which
were beautiful because
of the music, and because
of the red scratches, the inflamed
skin, which meant to me
that she had truly lived,
though my father said
the cats meant
she had no life.

Karen Berry taught me to play
Rush and Aerosmith.
Classical isn't everything, she'd say.
Karen Berry needed no one.
Karen Berry drove a beat up Honda
with a bumper sticker that said,
"Honk if you think I'm Jesus."
And I always wondered
if anyone honked. I always
wondered if, out there
on the highways, drivers
laid hard on their horns,
a terrible orchestra rising out
from steering wheels
as if to say *Yes, Karen Berry,*
you are the Lord our Savior.

The Tie That Binds

It's probably not good for you, your mother says,
her eyes scanning from your eyes to your belt.
She's worried your chest is bound too tightly,
says it's not natural, that she's concerned
about your health, your comfort. You're sixteen.
And there is solace in moving through a day
in pain—shoulders marked with bloodlines,
a red road of welts forming on the stomach.
It means you proceed through each moment
knowing that being who you are must hurt
if it is going to mean anything. You learn
this best in second grade when your nerves
get the best of you, when you bite
your tongue down to bleeding
in gym class. Mrs. Garafalo thinks
your tongue is gum, sends you
to the girls' locker room to write one hundred times
"I will not chew gum in gym class."
In the locker room, your hands shake,
the chalk makes the sound chalk makes,
you taste the blood in your teeth,
you imagine a world with no locker rooms,
you know your body will always be at half-mast.

Why didn't you tell her it wasn't gum? your mother asks.
And you hang your head, continue to peel the orange.
You learn how to survive in the wild, you learn
to feed the fire of your silence, to never open your palm,
never show what you're holding, what
truth is made natural in your trembling hands.
Perpetually out of breath, perpetually dying,
lungs pulled tight. But you will not die.
You will breathe slower, shallower.
You will bleed. And you will live.

Masculinity II

Tonguing that one loose tooth
as a child, trying to rid the mouth
of excess. Your heart
is the wrong machine
left by your parents
in the wrong repair shop.
We are all fools when
it comes down
to mechanics.

Being Queer in High School

Traveling through space, looking around the ship
knowing damn well not one of us was an astronaut
or knew anything about how to keep ourselves alive in space.

Chicken wire and long stairways,
like a hobby you don't want, old glue,
high tides, the pull of something better.

Lightning, no money, no movies,
a lobby you did not want to wait in,
the smell of the food court at the mall.

Listening to Motley Crew in your best friend's
orange Nova at the Mayfair Shopping Center,
the only girl baritone in the chorus.

The shame of the straight boy altos,
the time you pinned the freshman heavyweight
on the wrestling team. You didn't want to touch him.

Drawing stick figures of lesbian sex on the bathroom walls,
writing in the notebook no one saw, and later,
the smell of the pages catching fire. Even now,
you would burn the notebook again, turn want to ash.

Boyfriend, 1992

for Paul

January again and
what you remember
is one night riding
in the snow plow
you took him
into your mouth
willing perhaps
because of the snow
or because
you had spent all night
clearing away
what winter you could
you did not drive
you did not
ask for
the headlights off
or the ceasing engine
you just
as you could
considered him aching
considered him needing
to feel his night job
was useful
your mother used to say
how useful he was
all this pushing aside
of the snow
all repair
nothing glorious
about the new
she'd say
how the birds
took to their nests

you did love him
you were
for a moment
a girl
with a boy
who loved her.

Masculinity III

Perhaps you should make other things:
make songs out of sirens, make bridges,
make noise in the movie theater
and then duck down. You are always
ducking down as if to say,
It couldn't have been me
because I am not even here.

When I imagine you have a mother,
she is quizzing you on the planets,
and you are not listening. You don't
want the names for places, you want
the places themselves. You want
places to move around on your tongue
like a fine wine until you decide
to swallow them quick and whole.

Everything Is Everything

This was 1993, and because we were the cool kids,
we were hanging out in the mall parking lot
smoking Newports and listening to Earth, Wind, and Fire's
"Everything Is Everything" turned up full volume
in my first girlfriend's bright blue Chevy Cavalier.

We didn't yet know what was coming.
When you're sixteen and queer in the suburbs,
your world is a deadly and magical secret.
Your every move a beautiful subversion.
So we listened to old music, closed
our eyes and imagined some covert
queer kid in 1971 turning up the volume,
hearing the song for the first time—
the long groove of the intro, the repetition
Everything is everything, listen to me.

We knew we had always been here.
We knew we weren't the first queer kids
to park in the way back of the mall to kiss.
We knew we weren't the first to sign
our love notes with a boy's name
in case they were read aloud in class
or found by our parents.

Everything is everything, listen to me.
Earth, Wind, Fire. Long Island,
New York. The mall was six miles
from northern shoreline, though we
never much thought about living on an island.
We only thought about the life no one knew we had,
about empty parking lots, saving
our money for the motels
we could rent by the hour.

We only thought about our music
and moving the car
from one parking lot to another
at thirty-minute intervals so the mall cop
wouldn't pull up to the window,
shine his light into the car,
try to uncover us from the smoke,
try to steal our secret earth.

Notes on Matt Damon

On ratemyprofessors.com,
quite a few of my students suggest
that my class is hard and
that I look like Matt Damon.
Some students have even granted me
the infamous "hot chili pepper" rating
for looking like him.

It's hard to know how to interpret this.
After all, Matt Damon is indeed handsome,
and if my last words could be any words,
those words just might be, "Do you like apples?
Well, I got her number. How do you like them apples?"
to the middle school boys who bullied me.

I'm not from Boston, but the power of the accent does speak to me.
I wonder what more Matt and I might have in common,
other than our East Coast upbringings.
After all, he was born on October 8, a Libra,
and I am a solid "on-top-of-things" Capricorn.

My parents divorced when I was seven, and young Matt
was a whopping thirteen when his parents untied the knot.
I wonder, did he run into the woods in celebration?
Did he dream of the day he'd actually stop seeing his father's leather shoes
at the back door, did he refuse to speak in school,
did he dress up in girl's clothes or pretend he was the lead singer of girl bands
like Heart or Wilson Phillips or, even better, The Bangles?

Did he want to work with his hands but find his hands inadequate?
Did he want to be taller?
Did he wander the halls of his middle school with notebooks
full of love notes never slipped into the lockers of girls

who thought of him as harmless or never thought of him at all?
Did he ever eat an entire gallon of Cookies-N-Cream on prom night
while the rest of the neighborhood danced in their beautiful genders?
Did he major in English, like all us poets do,
because he believes language precedes action?
Did he ever listen to his mother crying
through the walls of his Cambridge home?
Did he like Latin when he learned Latin?
Did he know when he was taking Latin
that only kids that eventually go to Harvard (which he did) take Latin?
Did he drop out of Harvard because he wanted to be a movie star
or because the ivy walls seemed sinister,
or because he would have preferred to be the genius janitor
solving equations overnight,
the unsung hero,
the silent show-off,
the handsome but underrated underdog?

Did he love expensive gin?
Is that why he married a bartender?
Did he become a Red Sox Fan
the same way I became a Yankees fan—
because some inheritances we cannot turn down,
because our grandfathers' opinions about major league baseball
were more important than their opinions on racism, sexism, and war.
Did he ever want to be a soldier?
Did he know he'd grow up to gather white boy directors on HBO
and combo mansplain-whitesplain racism to Effie Brown?
Did he know what power and money and whiteness would make of him?
Did he know what teeth masculinity sprouts in the mouth?
What privilege he could not feel in the frightening woods of childhood?
Did I know? Did I know the pain and danger of my failed girl skin
was also the implicated safety of my white skin?

Did I know the tangled web we weave, Matt Damon,
with our white boy smiles and perceived objectivity,
with our hot chili peppers
and East Coast accents?
I don't want to be you, Matt Damon.
What can I do to stop being you—
to be some other kind of man,
the kind of man who, in the end,
knows when to sit down,
shut up and listen.

Part Two

Men Who Think I Am One of Them Speak
We know that guy, and he is not a rapist.

He wants me to feel included in the "we."
Us men, we know each other, know when
one of us is a rapist. This one is my friend,
maybe, or maybe we've patted one another
on the back the way men do. We do know
that guy. We have patted his back.
We have both pretended he was funny,
entered into the man pact whereby
complicity is an old t-shirt we wear
under our clothes. *She could say that*
about anyone, he goes on to say.
And he shifts his eyes to the side,
looking for the man in me to understand,
waiting for my half man body to show its worry.
His eyes widen, only a bit aggressively.
He wants me on the defensive team,
to anticipate the charge, to imagine
myself the man victim of the claim
that cannot be true because
we know that guy, and he is not a rapist,
said every man whose friend is a rapist.

Men Who Think I Am One of Them Speak
She really let herself go.

This story is hard to tell
when the men you love
insist a woman hold on
never
let herself go
never
let herself loose
never
let herself leave
never
let herself depart
never
let herself mobilize
never
let herself imagine
never
let herself grow
big enough to lift off
the runway
like a jet
full of fuel.

Men Who Think I Am One of Them Speak
Check out that ass.

When they say this,
there is always
in their voices
a sense of urgency like
that ass is the edge of a cliff.
And they could die
with one wrong step.

My father checked out
asses, thighs, any part
of any woman, never
any whole of any one.

*You are just like
your father* is something
distant relatives would say
to explain why he and I couldn't
get along. *Both such charmers.*
Both so stubborn.

Check out that ass.
Check out the way she
Check out her
Check out that
man who thinks
I am one of him
my father
my rootstock
what parts of me
rhizome underground,
spreading the way
this man who thinks

I might
be one of him
tells me to *check out*
that ass, and I am
checked out.

Masculinity IV

I am sometimes the notebooks
you wrote in as a child,
my whole body pressed
by the movement of your hand.

You tell me everything.
I hold your words in place.
I keep your history safe.

I am sometimes the yarn
you purl and knit, my whole
body tangled in webs.
You unravel me
row by row. You make
me into scarves, methodically
lead me through the
loops and pulls of my own body.

Men Who Think I Am One of Them Speak

You're not going to write poems about your kid now, right?

Says the famous man poet who
I am sure is only concerned about
my career, just concerned the birth
of my son will cause a sentimental
softening and my poems will
be swallowed by some narrator
who is someone's mother, even though
my son does not call me mom.

The speaker of poems, he believes,
cannot be the voice of someone's mother—
lines have to be crafted of some superior
notion of form, precision, the lock stop
of a line. And who can possibly do that
if their heart is half full of a child,
even though my son, like all of us,
is made of language, spoken into being.
So I let him be alive in the lines.
I write him again, ask him to be
the kind of man whose heart
is half full of something,
something other
than just his best work.

Men Who Think I Am One of Them Speak

Yeah but, you know, why is she bringing this up now?

This one said twice
once about
Christine Blasey Ford
once about
the student
whose instructor
told her what she could do
with her hands—
bringing this up now
is not the right time
to bring it up
have to bring it up
at the right time
just not
after it happens
or after you realize
what it is
or
after enough years
that the men who think
I am one of them
have to think back
to when they might
have done a thing
that should
not be brought up now
because now is not
the time to bring it up
now is not truth time
these two men
who said these two things
do not think now
is the right time

it's been too long
even they can't remember
if they've done
anything that
could be brought up
now, or ever.

Men Who Think I Am One of Them Speak

I forget you're a woman sometimes.

I do, too
except when
I don't
like when
I am afraid
of losing you
if I say
please no
please don't
forget where
I come from
those of us
who believe
we were ever
women
are tired
of all your
forgetting
your loss
of memory
your simple
equations
that reduce
any moment
to anything
less than
forever.

Masculinity V

While in life you should
not feel responsible
for such things, consider
you are holding up the sky
and need to prop up
its height. You move the sky
with your breath, but
you are not a God.
You are exactly yourself.
Lift the sky to its sky,
find the sky of the sky,
the breath of your breath.
Breathe in more than your lungs.

Men Who Think I Am One of Them Speak
You know what I'm saying, right?

Often said after
the sexist thing
when they see
my face is not
doing the thing
a man's face should
do when his buddy
says *she's a bitch*
you know
what I'm saying
right
she's a slut
you know
what I'm saying
right
she's smokin' hot
you know
what I'm saying
right
she's abrasive
you know
what I'm saying
right
she's got like
no sense of humor
like
you know
what I'm saying
right?

Men Who Think I Am One of Them Speak

Dude, we are going to have to fight them off with sticks.

He is my friend
and means
that my daughter
just born
is beautiful.
But it's him
I want
to punch
in the face
right now
him I want
to fight off
with a stick
but
he is my friend
of course
and means
that my daughter
just born
is beautiful
already
a temptress
a body to be
checked
out by some
of the men
who think I am
one of them
while she is
defended by men
of whom
maybe
I am one

and we will
fight them off
with sticks
and my daughter
will never be
her own
not here
not like this.

Masculinity VI

You want everyone to think
you're not shivering
so you pull off
your fear as mere motion.
Nicotine stains
and round yawns.
You're bored
with everyone's
commentary
so you go home,
wipe the ashes
from the ashtray
with your fingers,
let your hands
smell of ash
for days.
You always
love what
is leftover,
the scent
after the act,
the remains
you refuse
to bury.

Part three

Bathroom Poem

I was in a rush, no time
for my usual ladies' room routine.
No time to wait and hide in the stall
until the whole room clears out.

I tried to sneak past quickly.
I really did, skipped the handwashing,
bolted straight from the stall
to the swinging door. But she
steps in front of me so fast
I almost fall back. *You can't
be in here*, she says, her hand
poking a bit into the space between
my collarbone and my chest.

She's a lot smaller than me,
but the size of my shame is
giant—impossible to contain,
the congealed mass of it
awake in my stomach.

You can't be here, or anywhere
is what she means. I dodge
my way to the door and run.
I forget to tell her to fuck off.
I forget to explain my position.
I forget to tell her my gender.
I forget to say:

*Sometimes my partner (who I
sometimes call my wife) calls
me her husband.
I cook all the meals
I have this chest*

other people call breasts,
no penis to speak of other
than the one I wear
from time to time,
only when
explicitly asked. I am told
I have the testosterone level
of an eighteen-year-old boy.
My parents call me a daughter
and I don't hate it because
it's a very affectionate
misunderstanding. One
might say I am a man
on the inside, intersex,
intersection, inflection of
my voice low register,
lexicon woman.
The words I use
are my mother's,
except when I hear myself
say to my son
Do you understand me?
and then it is a man
who speaks, who tries
to deny the full extent
of his powerlessness.
And so: what bathroom
do you think I should use?

Give Us Your Pronouns

They say,
give us
your pronouns.
So proud
of themselves
for asking.
Give us your
pro nouns.
Tell us how
you would like us
to refer to you,
your pronouns
your for nouns
for people
for places
for things
the proper noun
for you is
your pronoun
which you should
give to us. Give
us your
pronouns. Please
help us
refer to you
correctly.
We don't
want to make
any mistakes
with your pronouns
which are yours
and you have them so
give us your pronouns
give us

this day
our daily
bread
give us time
give us
a bloodhound
with no sense
of smell.
Your pronouns
your canine
lost
in the woods.

Reading Queer

It's what it would look like
if a circle
could have four sides.

A young boyish girl
howls at a tree,
hoping the howling
will cause it to bloom.

Tears shaped like dragonflies
fall from the lines of her words,
which are wheels
inside a single tear,
tools we misuse
and misname.

A basket of berries
no one has come to claim.

The kettle whistling
the song of the body
gender will not leave
well enough alone.

Masculinity VII

You want to turn your arteries into vines,
the valves into sailor's knots. This is your plan,
to escape from your own body. Your syntax
a soft pulse. Put your fingers to your neck
to measure it, so you'll know if you survived the fall.

Deadlocked

The Nebraska Board of Education
member Maris Bentley says
we need to protect our kids
from the harmful queer agenda.
The board itself deadlocked,
three on three.

Maris Bentley fears
that "choose your own
bathroom" makes gender
"too loosey-goosey,"
like each urination
will become a choose your own
adventure—she's afraid
kids will change
their genders daily,
afraid the sexual predators
will come out of the woodwork
like dirty disobedient termites
gnawing at the thin panel
of values she's taught
her four kids,
her ten grandchildren,
the hundreds of students
to whom she has been
a counselor.

Maris Bentley,
there's so much I want to say,
but I know it will do no good.
You're deadlocked, after all,
like happened to me once,
driving through Pennsylvania

when a man's hands
were deadlocked into my throat
as I left a public restroom.

I can't read
the way you want me to,
Maris Bentley. My gender is
deadlocked, too, in the space
between man and woman,
chromosomes deadlocked,
hormones deadlocked,
body deadlocked,
haircut deadlocked,
others like me
locked dead in their bodies,
locked dead in your language,
locked
dead.

When Butches Shoot Pool

for Julie

Sometimes one of them goes overboard.
Sometimes one of them gets drunk.
Sometimes one of them starts a fight
with a woman who looks like Tony Danza.
Sometimes one of them sinks the cue ball.
Sometimes one of them gives the other the last cigarette.
Sometimes one of them becomes the other's father.
Sometimes one of them holds the pool stick like a rifle.
Sometimes one of them makes fun of other's side spin.
Sometimes one of them hits a three-cushion bank shot,
Sometimes one of them has the blue of the chalk on their fingertips
or the blue of the blue chalk in their blue eyes.
Sometimes one of them calls the other a sissy boy.
Sometimes one of them plays a sexist song
on the juke box and calls their partner "the wife."
Sometimes one of them slaps the quarters down on the table
like it's the very last pulsing left in their beating hearts.
Sometimes one of them imagines their rage contained by the triangle,
watches it crack open in the other's clean break.
Sometimes one them calls the shot by nodding their head
in the direction of the intended pocket.
Sometimes one of them is wearing the same cologne
they wore in high school.
But when the night is over,
when they've left the bar without yelling or fighting,
when they've left the last bills for the bartender,
when they've both spit on the city sidewalk,
when they've reached the fast food parking lot down by the river,
one of them would hold the other if they cried—
not that they cry,
just
if they did.

The Kill

To be a good assassin, you have to plan.
You don't hire a hitman, you have
to do this work alone. You must know
that gender hangs out in every crack
and divot on the whole earth,
and on whole bodies, and you will
have to figure out how to kill it
even as it is everywhere and nowhere.

You have to know gender does not like
to be noticed. And you might have to shove
its head in the sand and say,
"I thought you'd like that, gender."
You might have to say,
"Maybe you'll think twice
next time your fancy yourself
an excuse for bullying or weeping
or waiting or death itself."

You'll feel bad but won't apologize
for what you are planning to do.
Like a good assassin, you will do the job
quickly and invisibly. You will take gender
by the throat before it even knows you're there.
It's done that to you for years.
Consider it payback.

And when gender is gone,
we will not mourn it holy.
We will not visit its tombstone.
We will leave it in an unmarked grave.
We will do our best to forget
where we came from.

Religious Liberty Accommodations Act

Mississippi Senate,
don't feel too special.
Bosses have been
firing (at) us
long before your laws,
long before your clerks
at the frontlines
of the "marriage debate."

Oh, Mississippi Senate, it's cute, really.
How your bill puts its stamp
on something queers have always known,
that our bodies are built by legislation,
that we don't get to decide our own genders
or the genders of those we choose to fuck,
that our sex toys require more zoning laws
than your guns, that our bodies are made
of your bullets, manufactured to discipline,
marketed into the hands of your foot soldiers
whose names don't matter, only
their hands that write the law
as your first line of defense,
first ammunition.

Masculinity VIII

You made all of this from broken bottles.
I keep scraping my thumbs on the edges
of your pronouns. I keep bleeding.
You have no consistent grammar.
You just keep raising your glass.
You never know when to quit.

Thankfully, you will have taught me freedom within constraints

after a painting by Lari Pittman

My son's bones are flames,
his rib cage, flanks of fire,
his body a storm of heat.

I do not know what he will warm
or burn or bring to ash.

I try to show him
what his hands are for,
teach him to be both
the tree and the fire,
to burn holes
in bad arguments,
to take down
the slats of walls
his country builds—
however symbolic.

Some mornings,
when it's all too much,
he cries incessantly,
shoves his ember fingers
inside his mouth,
tries to contain his own heat,
to soothe its infinite motion
inside his jaw.

And I pick him up,
as parents are said to do.
I turn on the kitchen sink,
and we listen
to the sound
water makes inside

a steel pan. We
both imagine
what it would be like
to be made of water.

Your Father

Say Father, then, to no one,
Or say my father was, himself,
A house, or say each word's a house,
Some lit & some abandoned.
Larry Levis, *Winter Stars*

When they ask if I am your father,
tell them the day you were born
your heartbeat was a hundred moth wings
tapping against a porch light.
Tell them my body is a labyrinth,
say our hearts are two falling moons
inside the twin caverns of our chests,
say your breath is the content of my lungs,
say your DNA is not a strand of mine,
but your manhood is a strand of mine,
your curve ball, your sentences,
your fear, your spelling errors,
all strands of mine.

When they ask if I am your father,
say "I am your father," in the dark voice
of Darth Vader, or sing "I will be your father figure,
put your tiny hand in mine," like you're
the irreverent George Michael of the '80s.

When they ask if I am your father,
say you grew up in a town
with tornado sirens, say your
mother is a sucker for men
who are women who are also men.

When they ask if I am your father,
tell them how I taught you to *be* a man
by teaching you how *not* to be a man.
When they ask you if I am your father

say, in the unshakable calm
of your voice: *if that is what you mean,*
then yeah, she's my father.

Some Notes on Family

Some nights it is your own mother.
Some nights it could never be.
You create it
out of your stepfather's billiards table
and the time he rubbed his face full over
with mashed potatoes to illustrate he
was nothing like your actual father
who (while others would say "of course he doesn't")
hated you for your deep voice and ball caps.
Sometimes you revise it—
leave a brother behind,
take a scalpel to the family,
leave behind a clean hole
stitched with precision.
Sometimes the hole is a good one
however scarred, however broken.
You build it
even when you have no idea how.
You build it in places you never thought
you'd want to go, flat places,
places that are further from the ocean
than anyone should be. But your son is born there,
and your best friend shows up with a crock pot,
and that's how it works.
If you stop building you find
yourself staring into a milkshake
at a rundown fast food joint, thinking
there has to be someone I can call.

When I Imagine the Day of Your Birth

The air is a thin layer of skin pulled tight
to the point of breaking. The whole sky
is at the point of breaking. I imagine
myself at four holding my small arms
out to my dreaming father who does not
yet know he hates me, or at least, wants
to take me from myself. I have to think
my young body felt the shift, that perhaps
I did something for the first time that day,
used a word I had never spoken,
built a snow fort without the help of my brothers.

I do think I had been waiting for you,
not in the way a lover waits for the one,
but in the way a child waits for their first
bike ride in the neighborhood alone,
for the first moment of trusting themselves
to pedal to some freedom better than home.

Letter to My Grandfather

There is a small coffee shop you would not like.
The country is still at war.
I teach students to want what they do not yet want.
I've learned to care about the fish downstairs in the lulling tank.

The wood floors do not hold in heat.
There's garbage on the beach
where you taught me to throw a slow curve.
One might say I do a fair job caring for the plants,
for the house and our children
whose hair is a tangle of sunlight.
Your dog and your wife and your brothers are gone.

The politicians again with their mouths.
My body, again, a story I cannot tell.
I train myself not to want.
Spring and the trees are rising
from their own deaths

like they do this time of year
when I'm thinking of you
and your wooden rake.

The Hit Man

I'm a nine-year-old girl. All I can think about is Don Mattingly.
Mattingly was a no-frills hitter—something endlessly compelling
about how relaxed he was—his hands loose around the grip
of the bat, his eyes clear and meditative. He never stood still

after hitting a home run to admire it; he never strutted.
But people still called him "Donnie Baseball"
or sometimes "The Hit Man." I'd watch the Yankee games
holding my peewee Louisville Slugger. I'd mirror him

in the living room—my mother yelling from the kitchen,
"If you swing that bat in the house, I swear to Holy Lord."
I was careful. I'd wait until my mother was a safe distance
from the room. I'd make sure there was no chance of disaster.

I used the new camcorder held up to the television
to tape Mattingly's at-bats, so I could play them in slow motion.
But I was not Don Mattingly. At least not until Little League
when Brian's dad says to my dad—loud enough for me to hear

after I hit a single to right center, rounded first base,
and put my hands together for one single Mattingly clap,
she hits like Donnie. My body lights up in recognition.
I tell the librarian at school, Mrs. Sullivan, about my batting average.

"That's pretty impressive, sir," she says on a day I stayed
to laminate book covers in the back room—a job given
to only the most careful and efficient library aide.
Mrs. Sullivan only called me "sir" in private.

She'd come to the back room and say,
"How many books covered, sir?"
Or sometimes she'd walk me out to the late bus and say,
"See you tomorrow, sir."

Sometimes, even now, I dream I am marrying Mrs. Sullivan.
I am wearing a tie, the sharpest, simplest tie.
In the dream I am Donnie, the Hit Man, the kind of man
for whom being a man is nothing special, nothing whole.

A Toast to My Body at Forty-Two

Here's to the wide expanse of your shoulders,
your mother saying, *I gave birth to that broadness.*

Here's to your round belly digging itself
into the cold metal of your belt buckle.

Here's to your noise, low and deep,
breath long into the mouth, machine gun
sound of your piss to the water, or to the ground,
the cracked pleasure of your knuckles
popping in your nervousness and fear.

Here's to the live electrical wire of your facial hair,
your chaotic levels of testosterone. Here's to no eggs
through the fallopian tubes, hollow and gloriously useless.

Here's to you—my incoherent biology, bearer of bulk muscle and bone.

Here's to the sharpness of your twenty-twenty sight,
your snotty-nose winter colds,
your quick-to-puke stomach, your unwashed hands.

Here's to your fevers, your hunger.

Here's to that moment when you abandon me,
when, finally and perfectly, your strength
will do you no good.

Here's to the metal in you, steel body—
rock, paper, scissors—gatherer
of water, blood, and stone.

The Cloud Looks Like a Breaking Wave

And this one a blue-gray tunnel,
and this one an escape hatch to heaven.
And every cloud is my body—
one minute you think you know
what the image means, and the next
moment a seven-year-old exclaims,
"This one looks like a pine tree,"
or "This one is a bicycle wheel."

If only we lived in a world of
imaginative interpretation, if only
we were as forgiving of bodies
as we are of clouds.

What wonder we could all be
to each other, what grief
we would not suffer,
what joy as we said
to one another lying back
on the roof of the car,
"Your body looks like a waterfall,"
or "Yours looks like an upside-
down umbrella." And we'd smile
and say, "Yes, I see it now
if I just turn my eyes the same angle
as yours." This cloud looks like
a breaking wave, which means,
in the end, it will be broken,
water becoming itself again.

Masculinity IX

The body sees itself
as a window.
My lover touches
the part of me that's infinite.

This love has no memory of you.
This love has no body of you.
It's as if it's always been,
as if a forest.

I do things you could not
imagine me doing.
When I cannot find you
in the wooded fields,
in the shredded birch bark,
in the curved line of my palms,
I want only to be enough.

A Real Man Would Have a Gun

Acknowledgments

Grateful acknowledgment to the journals, books, and online publications that previously published many of the individual poems in this collection, including:

Academy of American Poets Poem-a-Day Series: "Men Who Think I Am One of Them Speak: *She really let herself go*"
Bodies Built for Game: The Prairie Schooner *Anthology of Contemporary Sports Writing,* edited by Natalie Diaz and Hannah Ensor: "The Hit Man"
Cherry Tree: "The Tie That Binds" and "Thankfully, you will have taught me freedom within constraints"
HeArt Quarterly: "When Butches Shoot Pool"
Nasty Women Poets: An Unapologetic Anthology of Subversive Verse, edited by Grace Bauer and Julie Kane: "Deadlocked"
The New Territory: "The Cloud Looks Like a Breaking Wave"
Ocean State Review: "Karen Berry" and "Being Queer in High School" (published as "Queer Adolescence")
Pittsburgh Poetry Review: "Notes on Matt Damon"
Recasting Masculinity: An Anthology, edited by Cedric Rudolph, RK Taylor, and Matt Ussia: "Men Who Think I Am One of Them Speak"
Shenandoah: "Mothers and Men"
Women of Resistance: Poems for a New Feminism, edited by Danielle Barnhart and Iris Mahan: "The Four Nights She's Gone"

I am humbled and grateful to be part of many writing communities that nurture my desire to write, reflect, and imagine the world (and myself) as transformative potentiality. I am very lucky to have no shortage of amazing writer friends in this world who remind me all the time that writing matters. I am so thankful to gabriel jesiolowski, whose deeply moving artwork appears on the cover of this book. I am particularly grateful to Brandon Som and Jennine Capó Crucet, without whom I would both write less and laugh less. I owe many thanks to all my graduate students and colleagues in the English Department at the University of Nebraska—Lincoln, especially Marco Abel, Hope Wabuke, Ava Winter, Joy Castro, Shari Stenberg, Timothy Schaffert, and Kwame Dawes, all of whom encouraged me and these poems at various stages. I am also so very grateful to have so many brilliant friends in Lincoln, Nebraska, who have supported me and loved me in a way that makes it feel possible to write a poem in the first place—especially Drew and Beth Jagadich, Mel Plaut, Katie Anania, Pete Capuano, James Brunton, and Emily Kazyak. Some of the poems in this book were difficult to write, and I do not know that I could have even thought some of these poems into being without the help of my therapist, Bryon, who has helped me understand myself as someone I might actually want to be. I am eternally grateful to my ride-or-die, Lauren Gatti, who has talked me through just about every moment of the last decade of my life. I am grateful every day to share a home and space with my two children, Max and Ollie. There is no place I have learned more about language and gender and grace than from these two remarkable human beings. I am so honored and humbled to be a parent to them. And finally, I am beyond grateful to my partner, Brie Owen—my home, my love, my anchor in every pain I've ever been lost in. There is so much I would not be brave enough to say without you.